SWEET BETSY FROM PIKE

SWEET BETSY FROM PIKE

Adapted and illustrated by

Roz Abisch and Boche Kaplan

THE McCALL PUBLISHING COMPANY

New York

For Frieda and Ben Kroop
Anna and Harry Spiegelman

SWEET BETSY FROM PIKE

Copyright © 1970 by Roz Abisch and Boche Kaplan

All rights reserved.

Published simultaneously in Canada by Doubleday Canada, Ltd., Toronto

Library of Congress Number: 75-104127

SBN8415-2006-2

First printing

Printed in the United States of America

The McCall Publishing Company

230 Park Avenue, New York, New York 10017

Did you ever hear tell of Sweet Betsy from Pike,
Who crossed the wide prairie with her husband Ike?
From Pike County, Missouri, so it is told,
They made their way westward, prospectin' for gold.

They loaded their wagon, and hitched up the horse,
They mapped out their route, and then set off on course;
With two yoke of cattle, a large yaller dog,
A tall Shanghai rooster, and one spotted hog.

Waving, "Good-bye, Pike County, farewell for a while,
We'll come back again when we've found our gold pile."

Way out on the prairie, at the end of one day,
They threw a big party, and Betsy was gay;
She sang, and she shouted, and skipped o'er the plain,
In a Pike County reel with the whole wagon train.

Singing, "Good-bye, Pike County, farewell for a while,
We'll come back again, and we'll do it in style!"

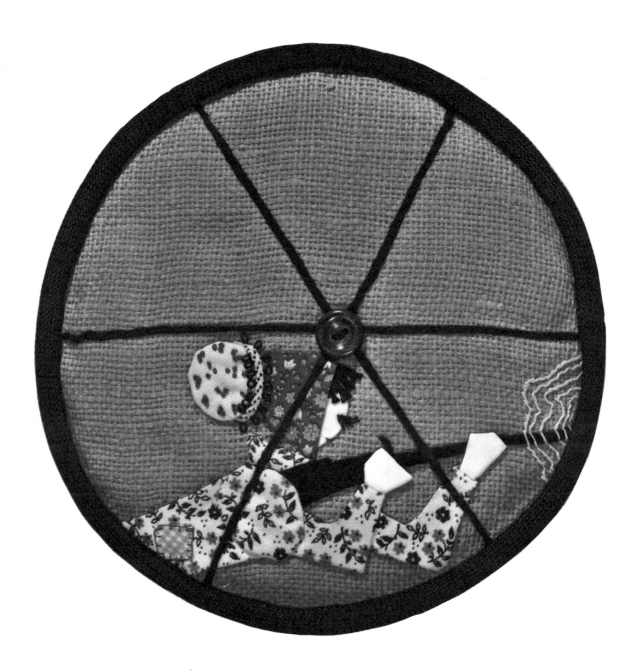

The trip was going well and spirits were high,
When a shower of arrows fell from the sky!
Behind the front wagon wheel Betsy did crawl,
And there she fought Injuns with musket and ball.

Betsy's wagon tipped over, and crash! hit the ground,
Her yard goods and ribbons flew out all around;
They tripped the poor Injuns all over the plain,
And Betsy was cheered by the whole wagon train.

Saying, "Good-bye, Pike County, farewell for a while,
We'll travel on westward, mile after mile."

But the journey grew tougher, the cattle grew weak,
Ike's bones were so tired, they started to creak;
He staggered, and stumbled and fumbled his way,
Along the rough, rocky road to Califor-nay.

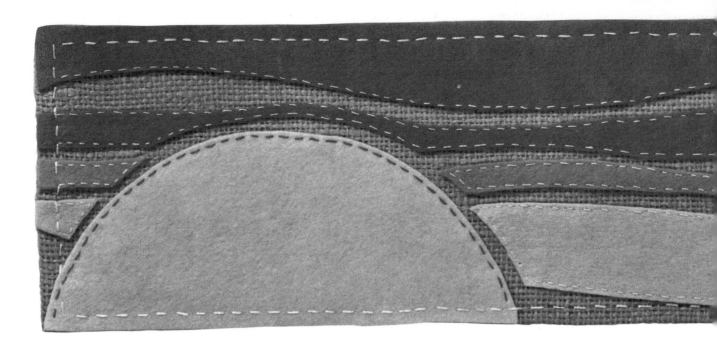

They reached the hot desert, but Betsy pushed on,
Though the wagon broke down, and the food was near gone;
Ike said, "Dear Pike County we'll come back to you."
Snapped Betsy, "You'll go by yourself, if you do!"

The great rolling desert was burning and bare,
And Ike feared the danger awaiting him there;
Sweet Betsy would not even stop for a rest,
But nagged Ike and dragged Ike on toward the west.

Crying, "Good-bye, Pike County, farewell for a while,
Since we've come this far, we'll not go back a mile."

They camped on the prairie for weeks upon weeks,
They swam the wide rivers, and crossed mountain peaks;
In order to get their old wagon to ride,
They had to keep tossing things over the side.

One morning they finished the last of the food,
The rooster grew hoarse, and the cattle just mooed;
Ike got more discouraged, and Betsy got mad,
The dog wagged his tail and looked wonderfully sad.

Weak and thirsty, poor Betsy crawled to a stream,
And there found the answer to her fondest dream;
Instead of plain water, running down clear and cold,
The stream overflowed with nuggets of gold.

Long Ike and Sweet Betsy then staked out their claim,
They worked long and hard for fortune and fame;
Ike mined so much gold, before the year's end.
There was more than even Sweet Betsy could spend.

Singing, "Good-bye, Pike County, we've done it at last,
This gold mine is ours, and we're getting rich fast!"

Then Betsy decided to buy a new gown,
So she went round the bend to the gold strike boom town;
There Ike bought her beads and bracelets and rings,
A solid gold shovel, and other fine things.

They built a fine house with room for the dog,
A barn for the cattle, a pen for the hog,
A roost for the rooster made out of pure gold,
And there they still live, as this tale is told.

Saying "Good-bye, Pike County, we send you our best,
We'll come back again when we're tired of the west."

Sweet Betsy From Pike

Chorus

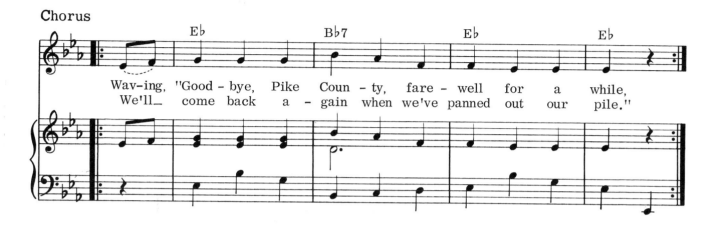

Wav-ing, "Good - bye, Pike Coun - ty, fare - well for a while,
We'll_ come back a - gain when we've panned out our pile."

NOTE:

SWEET BETSY FROM PIKE was adapted from a ballad written by an unknown singer of the 1850s. Sweet Betsy was the belle of the Gold Rush of 1849. Her fame traveled through Utah, Wyoming, Missouri, Colorado, and Nevada to California. Her story embodied the difficulties and fears and hopes of the westward-bound immigrants who added new verses to her tale as they journeyed cross country to seek their fortunes.